A story of ideas and hope

To everyone who creates a good tomorrow

JACKIE FRENCH

To Prabha, Annie and Rachel who all look just as
fantastic in their ugg boots as they do in their gumboots

SUE DEGENNARO

THE TOMORROW BOOK

JACKIE FRENCH

Illustrated by

SUE DEGENNARO

Angus&Robertson
An imprint of HarperCollins*Publishers*

Once upon a time – or maybe just tomorrow –
a little prince crawled
into the palace library.

The little prince loved books.

BUT

SOMEHOW

the world outside the palace never looked like the places he imagined as he read.

MPUTER
ATM
7

'Why?' he asked the butler.

'That's REAL LIFE, your royal highness,'

said the butler kindly.

'Well ...'

said the little prince.

'I think real life could be improved.'

One day, the king and queen packed up the royal campervan and left the little prince in charge.

The local kids decided it was time to visit.

'Please can you help us! Our vegie garden is dying.

We can't fill up our swimming pool.

There's not even enough water to have a bath!'

'Well ...'

said the little prince.

'Let's see.'

bio
filter

‘You can collect the water from your roof, use it over and over again inside and then clean it to grow your vegies.

You can even condense water from the air – enough to fill your swimming pool!’

Soon the kids were back again.

'We need better ways to get around.
We're sick of sitting in the car and petrol is **SO** expensive!'

'Well …' began the little prince.

AVENUE
BOULEVAR
FRESH PASTA - RAVIOLI
Victoria
Fax (03)

'You could run your car – and your whole house – by using the sun or the wind.

Why not use solar power and helium to **FLY** instead!'

But

that

night ...

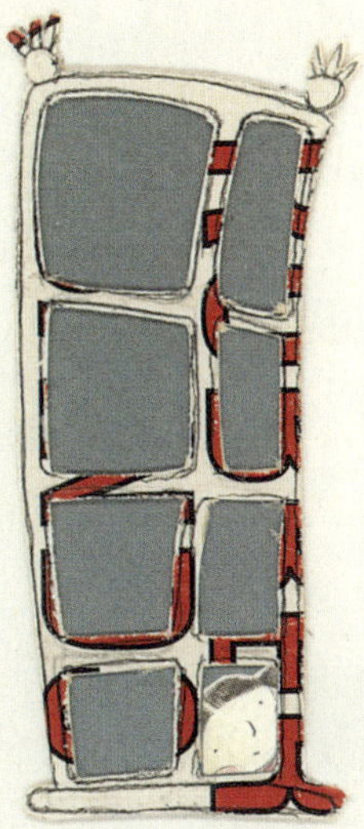

Psst!

'It's me again.

Mum reckons my room's a mess, but you should see the junk grown-ups leave all over the place!'

bike repair
open
We fix it all...

'Well ... repair stuff and use old things to make new things.

Hard plastic made from plants will turn back into soil one day – you could use it to make plastic spaceships, bicycles, and computers!'

The prince hadn't been back at the palace long when ...

'Ahem ... **MORE** visitors, your royal highness,' said the butler.

The little prince grinned.

'I think I know why **YOU'RE** here ...'

Water tank
Water tank
Water tank
Water tank

He went over to the window and shouted out loud,

'WE NEED TO SHARE THE WORLD!

We must find homes for animals, with lots of trees, and safe ways for them to move around!'

J
K

The palace library was always busy now.

'It's going to be the **BEST** world soon,' cried the little prince,

and the sound of children's voices everywhere joined in.

'MAYBE...'

TOMORROW!

Moon ride

AUTHOR'S NOTE

This book was written on a solar-powered computer, in an orchard where wombats and other wildlife wander, while I ate scones cooked in my solar oven and apricots grown on moisture captured from the night air.

All the 'new' ideas in this book have already been invented, except those on the last page, where dreams are still being made into real life. Some are even happening now, like our solar oven, and orchard designed to capture moisture and let wildlife share the land.

Our world could have luxurious floating 'zeppelins' instead of cramped polluting aeroplanes; wind- and solar-powered ships to zap us across oceans; cars and houses with walls and roofs made from solar cells; and even a space needle so we could ride an elevator up past earth's gravity to the stars.

We could capture the CO_2 that's warming our planet by making everything from computers to cars from hard plastics made from farm waste, prawn shells, garbage and even sewage. Various plants and bacteria can make polluted land safe and we could make the deserts bloom with seeds in capsules that won't break open unless it rains.

Our streets, schools and parks could be filled with fruit for anyone to pick, and also be used for markets where neighbours could swap produce and things they no longer need. Our tall buildings could have wildlife sanctuaries on their rooftops, and birds nesting in the vines growing on their walls. Every house could 'condense' moisture from the air to be used to cool or warm the house, as well as for chooks and vegies in the backyard.

Humans have already triumphed over far worse problems than we have now. We've even survived ice ages. When times get tough humans are capable of the most extraordinary dreams and teamwork. Maybe tomorrow you'll ride a dinosaur to school, or fly on solar-powered wings.

Tomorrow is going to be fun.

ILLUSTRATOR'S NOTE

The illustrations in this book were all created from recycled materials. I limited myself to paper found only within the confines of my house. Each image is made up of a collection of packaging found in my kitchen cupboards, such as tea-bags, flour packets and match-boxes. I've also used traces of envelopes from mail delivered to my house. Other pieces of paper I collected years ago and have held onto, along with stray cards from a playing deck.

Unlike Jackie, I live with my family in the inner city. To get around each day, we use bike lanes as well as public transport. We have a vegie patch in our back yard and it is watered from water collected from our roof. We have chickens who spend more time in our neighbour's back yard than at home and a guinea pig that mows our front lawn and fertilises it at the same time. Our front yard is filled with native trees and grasses that thrive in the warm summer months.

I, too, dream of tomorrow with a sense of excitement and wonder, its possibilities endless, and I smile at the thought of one day cycling into the city to meet a wombat or two for scones and tea.

Angus & Robertson
An imprint of HarperCollins*Publishers* Australia

First published in Australia in 2010
by HarperCollins*Publishers* Australia Pty Limited
ABN 36 009 913 517
www.harpercollins.com.au

HarperCollins*Publishers*
25 Ryde Road, Pymble, Sydney, NSW 2073, Australia
31 View Road, Glenfield, Auckland 0627, New Zealand
A 53, Sector 57, Noida, UP, India
77–85 Fulham Palace Road, London, W6 8JB, United Kingdom
2 Bloor Street East, 20th floor, Toronto, Ontario M4W 1A8, Canada
10 East 53rd Street, New York NY 10022, USA

National Library of Australia Cataloguing-in-Publication entry

French, Jackie.
The tomorrow book / Jackie French; illustrator, Sue deGennaro.

ISBN 978 0 7322 8939 3 (hbk.)
ISBN 978 0 7322 8940 9 (pbk.)

For primary school age.
deGennaro, Sue

A823.3

Cover and internal design by Natalie Winter
The illustrations in this book were created using watercolour, gouache and pencil in combination with recycled materials as collage.

Colour reproduction by Graphic Print Group, Adelaide.
Printed and bound in China by Phoenix Offset on 105gsm Oji Woodfree.
Oji Woodfree used by HarperCollins*Publishers*, is a natural, recyclable product made from wood grown in sustainable plantation forests.

5 4 3 2 1 10 11 12 13

If you'd like to know more about
the inventions in this book, go to:
http://harpercollins.com.au/resources/teachers.aspx
where Teachers Notes can also be found.